I DARE YOU!

Contents

Diana Bentley

Story illustrated by
Steve May

Before Reading

In this story

 Lee

Emma

Tricky words

- better
- higher
- what
- care
- faster

Introduce these tricky words and help the reader when they come across them later!

Story starter

Emma and Lee are twins. They are great friends but one twin is always trying to be better than the other twin. One day, they went to an adventure playground. Lee said that he could go higher and faster than Emma.

Showing Off

"I am better than you," said Lee.

"I can go higher than you," said Lee.

"So what?" said Emma,
"I don't care!"

"I can go faster than you," said Lee.

Do you like going down steep slides?

"So what?" said Emma.
"I don't care!"

"I can go faster than you," said Lee.

"So what?" said Emma.
"I don't care."

"I can go higher than you," said Lee.

"So you can!" said Emma.

"You can go higher," said Emma, "but you can't get down!"

Quiz

Text Detective

- How was Lee showing off?
- Have you ever shown off? What happened?

Word Detective

- **Phonic Focus:** Initial phonemes

  Page 6: Find a word beginning with the phoneme 'f'.
- Page 9: What does Emma actually say to Lee?
- Page 12: Find a word that means 'cannot'.

Super Speller

Read these words:

so   am

Now try to spell them!

HA! HA! HA!

Q Why did the chicken cross the playground?

A To get to the other slide.

13

Before Reading

Find out about

- Some amazing daredevil equipment

Tricky words

- trampoline
- high
- would
- walkway
- climbing

Introduce these tricky words and help the reader when they come across them later!

Text starter

You might have had a go on a trampoline, or a slide, a walkway or a climbing wall, but some people can do amazing daredevil feats on this equipment. Would you try that?

Would You Dare?

Have you been on a trampoline?

Some gymnasts can jump as high as 9 metres!

On a trampoline you can go high.

But would you try this?

Have you been on a slide?

On a slide you can go fast.

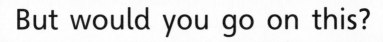

But would you go on this?

Have you been on a walkway?

On a walkway you can
go fast.

But would you try this?

Have you been on a climbing wall?

On a climbing wall you can climb high.

But would you go on this?

Quiz

- What are some of the daring things described in this text?
- What is the most daring thing you have ever done?

Word Detective

- **Phonic Focus:** Initial phonemes
  Page 15: Find a word beginning with the phoneme 'y'.
- Page 18: Find a word that means 'quickly'.
- Page 20: Find a word that is made of two little words.

Super Speller

Read these words:

on   go

Now try to spell them!

HA! HA! HA!

Q What's big and scary and goes up and down?

A A monster on a trampoline.